A Pup Grows Up

SALLY FOSTER

Photographs by the author

DODD, MEAD & COMPANY   New York

To Ben

The author wishes to express her gratitude to the people whose dogs appear in the book:

Basset Hound—Slippery Hill Bassets, Timber Ridge Bassets; Border Collie—Jack Price, Ann Russell Jones, Lewis Pulfer; Dalmatian—Robert Zuern, Sybil Dukehart, Howard County Fire Station 8; Springer Spaniel—Bonnie Bosley, Roger Birckhead; Jack Russell Terrier—Julie Colhoun; Great Dane—Mary Jones, Ellie Shapiro; German Shorthaired Pointer—Bruce and Monica Klinefelter; Saluki—Carol Smith, Janis Copenhaver; English Setter—Werner Mueller, Jerry Beal, Marie Scarlett; German Shepherd—Bea Connelly, Baltimore City K-9 Corps; Italian Greyhound—Joan Jacobauski; Longhaired Dachshund—Mary Howell, Polly Nelson; Chesapeake Bay Retriever—Nat Horn; Toy Poodle—Nancy Minkoff, Eric Braun/Ringling Bros. and Barnum & Bailey Combined Shows, Inc.; Mutt—Harford County Humane Society, Schuler School of Fine Arts.

1   2   3   4   5   6   7   8   9   10

Library of Congress Cataloging in Publication Data

Foster, Sally, date
   A pup grows up.

   Summary: Text and photographs introduce fifteen breeds of dogs,
presenting them as pups and as working adults.
   1. Dogs—Juvenile literature. 2. Dog breeds—Juvenile literature.
[1. Dog breeds. 2. Working dogs]
I. Title.
SF426.5.F67   1984   636.7'1   83-25474
ISBN 0-396-08314-5

A Pup Grows Up

Basset Hound

A Basset Hound pup can grow up…

to be a good hunting dog. Bassets are scent hounds. They run with their noses close to the ground to pick up the smell of rabbits or any other game.

Bassets are slow, steady hunters. They may
hunt alone or in packs. When they find the
scent, they sing out in loud, clear voices.

Basset hounds have loose-fitting coats and long, velvety ears. They are known for their strength and sturdiness.

Border Collie

Many Border Collies grow up...

to be working dogs. They round up the sheep or cattle on a farm. They have a natural herding instinct and like to see everything in its place. Sometimes they round up ducks and geese, too!

A Border Collie uses its eyes almost to hypnotize the sheep. It stares directly at the leader of the flock, while gently creeping forward. If one sheep breaks away, the Border Collie quickly darts around to head off the escape.

Border Collies are considered one of the best sheep dogs. Their name "collie" comes from the Gaelic word *colly*, meaning sheep.

Dalmatian

Many years ago Dalmatian puppies grew up…

to be coach dogs. They would follow along behind carriages to warn of approaching robbers. Their sharp ears could pick up the sound of hoofbeats that were very far away. They would also shoo farm animals out of the road.

Dalmatians were popular as firemen's mascots. They would ride atop the horse-drawn fire engines. Some firehouses still have them today.

When first born, Dalmatians are white.
The black spots come later. They are
intelligent dogs, easily trained.

Springer Spaniel

Springer Spaniel puppies are often trained…

to be bird dogs. Staying
close to the hunter, they
push forward through the
dense undergrowth where
pheasants, ruffed grouse,
and woodcock like to hide.
Long hair on their legs and
ears helps protect them
from briers.

Springer Spaniels can smell the birds. When they find them, they chase them out. A shot rings out and the dog awaits the hunter's command to fetch the bird. Springer Spaniels have very gentle mouths. They can carry a live bird without hurting it.

These dogs are known for their long,
floppy ears, wistful eyes, and friendly
wagging tails. They have very good
dispositions.

Jack Russell Terrier

Jack Russell Terriers are…

true working dogs. They are bred to hunt. They wriggle down holes looking for small animals.

Sometimes they will chase squirrels up trees or try to catch minnows in a stream. Jack Russells are best at killing rats. Many farmers, especially in England, use them instead of cats to keep their barns free of rats.

These dogs are mostly white. They
can be seen easily by hunters and won't
be mistaken for a fox. The Jack Russell
Terrier makes a first-class pet and
family dog.

Great Dane

Great Danes grow up…

to be very big dogs! They make good guard dogs, and yet they are surprisingly gentle. Great Danes are smart. Some have been taught to carry baskets, while others have learned on their own to unlatch doors.

Great Danes were used many years ago to
hunt wild boar in Germany. They also
guarded castles in European countries,
just the way they guard homes today.

The Harlequin Great Dane, with black
spots against a white background, was
prized as a coach dog. Today, Great Danes
are most often affectionate family pets.

German Shorthaired Pointer

When these German Shorthaired Pointer
puppies are older…

they may hunt for birds on land or near
the water. With their noses held high, they
sniff the air to pick up the scent of quail,
pheasant, or woodcock.

Once a German Shorthaired Pointer finds
a bird, it remains still, with its nose
pointed toward it. It is able to stand in
one position for up to two hours.

In some areas, these dogs are used to track rabbits, foxes, and deer. In the Midwest, they have been used to hunt mountain lions. German Shorthaired Pointers are very playful dogs.

Saluki

When these Salukis grow up...

they may learn to run in races. Salukis are sight hounds. They hunt by sight rather than by scent. They are taught to chase after a lure or plastic bag tied to a moving wire. The lure zips along a zigzag path and the dogs race to try to catch it. Sometimes they do.

Salukis have thick hair between their toes
which protects them from rough rocks
and stones. A long time ago, they were
used by the Arabs to hunt gazelles, which
are the swiftest of all antelopes.

With graceful, thin bodies and long legs, they are built for speed. Salukis can run faster than forty miles an hour.

English Setter

Can you guess what this English Setter
will do…

when he grows up? Maybe he will go
hunting for quail and pheasant hiding in
corn stubble. An English Setter uses its

sharp nose to find the birds. When it does,
it becomes still as a statue. This lets the
hunter know exactly where the bird is.

English Setters are graceful and intelligent dogs. They have mild, friendly dispositions, and are devoted to their masters.

German Shepherd

When these German Shepherd puppies grow up…

they may become police dogs. They will be taught to climb ladders and jump over walls, so they will be able to help policemen track down criminals.

These dogs have an excellent sense of smell and are often used to sniff out bombs or locate hidden, illegal drugs. They are brave, loyal, and intelligent.

German Shepherds are also used as guard dogs and Seeing-Eye dogs. But they make devoted family pets and companions.

Italian Greyhound

Italian Greyhound puppies grow up…

to be good house pets. But watch out, they
may play tug-of-war with your socks and
your best shirt. Italian Greyhounds hardly
ever sit still. They are always moving—like
wind-up toys.

These dogs have a funny habit. They don't like their backsides to touch the cold ground, so they often hold their rear ends up in the air.

Italian Greyhounds are miniature versions
of the racing Greyhound. They are Toy
dogs, and only weigh about eight pounds
when grown. They are very gentle, with
large expressive eyes.

Longhaired Dachshund

Dachshunds were originally bred for hunting...

but nowadays they are most often family pets. Still, a strong hunting instinct remains, and Dachshunds that live in the country will go off in search of animals that live underground. Down a hole they go, looking for mice, moles, woodchucks.

Owners of a Dachshund jokingly say that it
is a dog that the whole family can pet at
the same time. A bold, alert dog, it makes
a good watchdog and city pet.

Chesapeake Bay Retriever

When this Chesapeake Bay Retriever
puppy grows up…

perhaps he will be a hunting dog. This dog's main job is to bring back the ducks once they are shot. The hunter yells, "Fetch!" and the dog plunges into the icy, choppy water. These dogs have been known to retrieve as many as 300 ducks in a single day.

Chesapeake Bay Retriever coats are
chocolate brown to a faded tan. They
blend in easily with their surroundings.
The dog has two coats—an oily outer coat
and a woolly under coat—that protect it
from the cold water. With one good shake,
it is almost dry.

Chesapeake Bay Retrievers are one of the few truly American dogs—a breed developed in this country.

Toy Poodle

When this Toy Poodle grows up...

maybe he will be a circus dog. Poodles are very intelligent and eager to please. They can easily learn to do tricks like jumping through hoops, skipping rope, walking on their hind legs, or turning somersaults. They are lively dogs and sometimes they act like clowns. They seem to love applause.

Poodles come in different sizes—Standard, Miniature, and Toy. The large poodles were used to retrieve ducks. Their curly coats were clipped to allow them to move easily through the water. But tufts of hair were left here and there to keep the dogs from getting too cold. Today, the practice is continued.

Toy poodles seem to enjoy the company of humans, rather than that of other dogs.

Mutt

A mutt might grow up…

to live in an artist's studio. This one is named Crown Prince Rudolf, which is a very fancy name for a dog of mixed background. He is a dog model and sits quietly while having his picture painted.

Mutts are sometimes called mongrels.
They are a mixture of two or more breeds.
They are by far the most popular of all
dogs. They are generally loyal and
devoted, and their owners will say there
are no other dogs like them.